GOODNIGHT, LITTLE DOCTOR

BETTY NGUYEN, MD · BRANDON PHAM, MD

First paperback edition June 2023

Book design by Betty Nguyen & Brandon Pham

ISBN 978-1-957557-14-4 (paperback)

Printed in the United States of America

Published by Black Phoenix Press

www.mdforkids.org

To the friends and family who have supported and loved us unconditionally, and to the mentors who have guided and taught us more than we could have imagined:

Thank you.

Betty & Brandon

Goodnight, little doctor. It's time for you to rest.
All doctors need sleep to perform at their best.

08:00

Since dawn, you've helped many patients today,
keeping their illnesses and symptoms at bay.

You've chosen such a special and noble career.
Your hard work will take you far — that's clear!

Put your patients first, wherever you go.

Here are the lessons every doctor should know.

Every doctor needs empathy, skill, and expertise.
But healing is more than just treating the disease.

If all you do is cure, then your job is not complete!
Patients are people, not just symptoms to treat.

You make a difference, no matter how big or small,
for healing others is the greatest privilege of all.

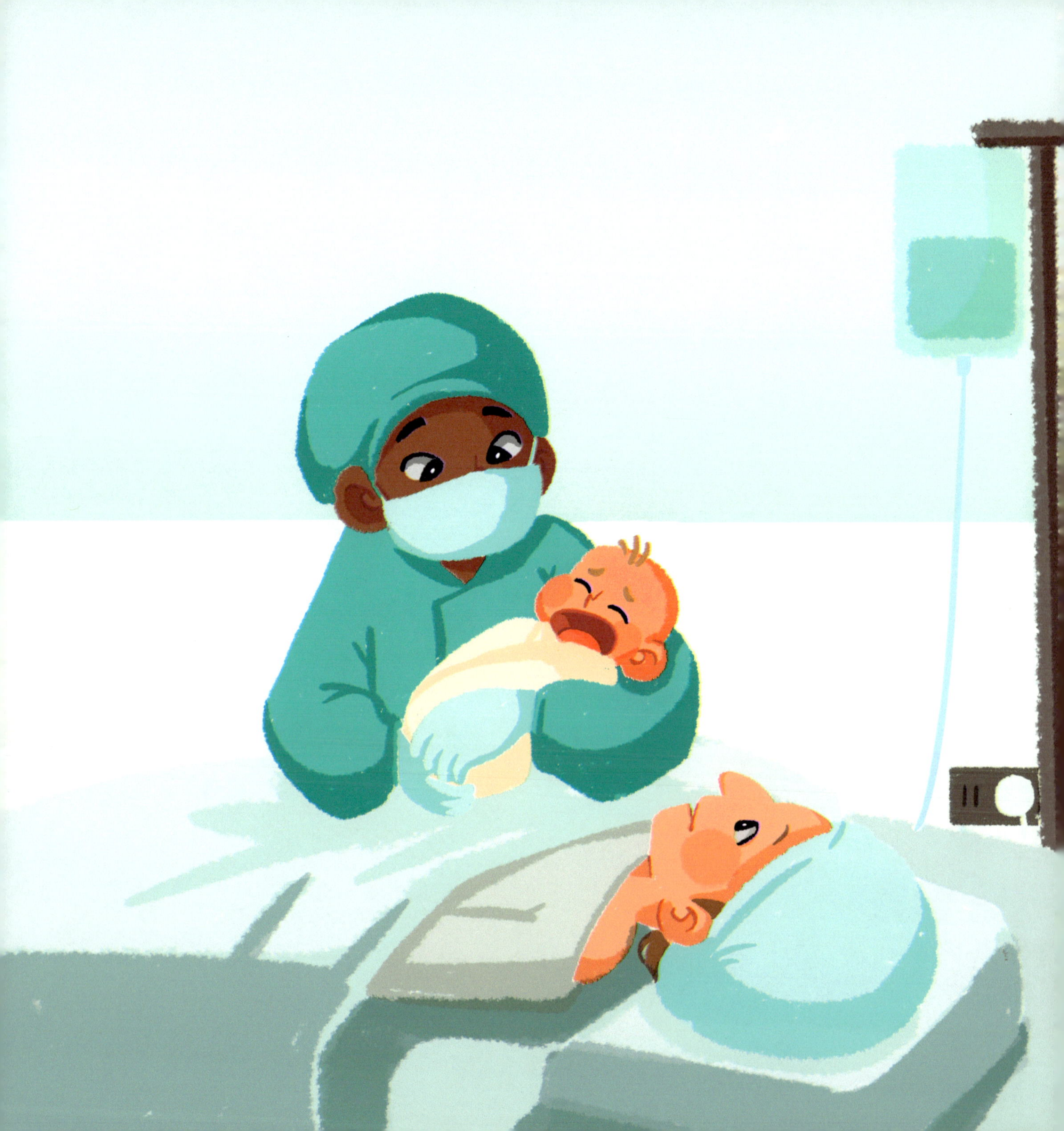

You interact with patients from all walks of life, during their biggest joys and moments of strife.

Treat patients with utmost kindness and respect.
That's more important than always being correct.

There will be some answers you simply don't know.

Remember your limits, be humble, and grow.

As a doctor, you can't avoid every mistake,
but always tell patients about any you make.

HOSPITAL

Your sacred bond with patients is built upon trust!
Having the highest level of integrity is a must.

HOSPITAL
P

There are no limits to what you can achieve.
Remember to dream big and to always believe!

Today, you've embodied these lessons and more.
These will make you the best doctor, I'm sure!

But now it's time to put your stethoscope away.
You deserve a break from all your duties today.

Close your eyes and let your mind unwind.
Leave all your thoughts and worries behind.

Goodnight, little doctor. I hope you sleep tight.
May your dreams be filled with joy tonight.

THE END

About the Authors

Betty Nguyen, MD

Betty is a physician specializing in dermatology. She was born in Southern California but spent much of her childhood in Georgia, where she grew up on a chicken farm. Betty studied Biology at UCLA, where she was a Gates Millennium Scholar, and earned her MD from UC Riverside on a full-tuition scholarship. Outside of work, Betty is a certified yoga instructor and licensed scuba diver. She also enjoys journalistic writing and cycling.

Brandon Pham, MD

Brandon is a physician specializing in ophthalmology. He was born and raised in Southern California. Brandon studied Microbiology, Immunology, and Molecular Genetics at UCLA, where he was a Barry Goldwater Scholar, and earned his MD from Stanford. He is passionate about medical education for students of all ages. In his free time, Brandon enjoys traveling, playing tennis, and performing card magic tricks.

Check out the rest of the books in our series!

Website: mdforkids.org
Instagram: @md.for.kids

Made in United States
Cleveland, OH
18 December 2025

29111577R00026